Islam Explained

Islam
Explained

TAHAR BEN
JELLOUN

THE NEW PRESS

NEW YORK

English translation of Islam Explained by Franklin Philip
© 2002 by The New Press
All rights reserved.
No part of this book may be reproduced, in any form,
without written permission from the publisher.

Published in the United States by The New Press, New York
Distributed by Perseus Distribution

ISBN 978-1-56584-897-9 (pbk.)
CIP data available

The New Press was established in 1990 as a not-for-profit alternative to the
large, commercial publishing houses currently dominating the book publishing industry. The New Press operates in the public interest rather than
for private gain, and is committed to publishing, in innovative ways,works
of educational, cultural, and community value that are often deemed
insufficiently profitable.

www.thenewpress.com

Book design by Ellen Cipriano

Composition by dix!

Printed in the United States of America

4 6 8 10 9 7 5 3

Contents

Islam Explained

Preface to the
American Edition

Despite its growth in the world, Islam is still misunderstood, and often grasped only as a caricature. For most of the European and American public, the image of Islam is negative. These past few years, people have been talking about it only in connection with dramatic occurrences and catastrophes (assassinations, terrorist attacks) as if this religion engendered only conflicts whose backdrop is one of fanaticism and intolerance. Most Americans first became aware of Islam either through the emblematic figure of Malcolm X or through the seizure of American soldiers as hostages in Iran. Indeed, it was with Khomeini's Iranian revolution in 1979 that Islam erupted in the world media as a political force. This religion, which in Arabic means "submission to peace," seemed to be a violent tornado that has promoted war rather than peace.

Since then, the mixture into Islam of the various elements of revolution, obscurantism, terrorism, and opposition to the West have increased and ended up constructing a hateful image of this religion and hence its followers. Certainly, a few days after September 11, the president of the United States made some gestures of reconciliation with the American Islamic community. He asked people not to confuse Islam with terrorism. But there were acts of aggression against Arabs and Muslims in September, and even against some Indians believed to belong to the Muslim religion. In this kind of situation, symbolic gestures are inadequate. It is for this reason that this book may prove valuable. It does not foster confusion, nor does it add further fuel to the conflicts. Quite the reverse, it explains and informs in the hope that this religion may no longer be diverted from its true path for political ends, purposes that foster the love of death more than the love of life and respect of others.

The men who attacked America on September 11, 2001, were in effect attacking Islam itself as a religion, a culture, and a civilization. They disfigured and betrayed it, for nowhere in the Islamic texts does it say that you must commit suicide while killing as many people as possible. In Islam, suicide is prohibited and punished in the beyond. Those who organized and planned these dreadful attacks have first and above all dealt a very serious blow to Islam and the world's Muslims. It has made them accomplices in a tragedy that nothing could justify. This was how it was experienced by the Muslim people, notably in several Arab countries. At the start, it is true, there were a few individuals who expressed their "joy" at the news of these slaughters. But these fools represented a minority that was ignorant of the gravity of such an event and confused the legitimate criticisms that could be made of American foreign policy (especially in the Near East) with "divine revenge," a revenge that killed innocent people.

Why this short book just now? For a simple reason: I have heard my own children repeat some inane remarks about Islam. I told myself that if Islam is misunderstood even in my own family, and if I who am a Muslim didn't know how to give my children proper instruction, what must it be like in other families? Then I read or reread some books written by specialists. In France, where Islam is the country's second most popular religion, there is an old tradition of orientalism concerning Islamic culture and civilization. I had to extract the essentials and present them simply, clearly, and above all objectively for young readers or adults. There was no question for me of persuading the reader of the accuracy of the prophet Muhammad's message or to get him to take up this religion. This is not a militant book. It is the book of a father who, talking to his children, would like to talk to all children everywhere. No question for me of writing a work of proselytism or of defending Islam because of its misrepresentation and misappropriation by terrorists. On the other hand, what I am seeking to do is to tell the story of Islam as it is recounted in serious books, to present it as something belonging to the universal heritage of humanity.

I have told the story of the prophet Muhammad and the birth of Islam as a tale. A magic story. Next I had to relate the history of the Arabs, and particularly their spreading influence over the world at the time when the spirit of curiosity and openness was the essential dynamic of their existence. Indeed, so open were they to other cultures, so widely did they translate the works of other civilizations, that they led the world in science, in intelligence, and in wisdom. As soon as they began fighting over political power, they neglected their culture, and their civilization began to decline.

What I would say to American readers today is that beyond the knowledge we may have of Islam, beyond this desire to know the other, the foreign, there is the need to keep the doors of one's own culture open. We can enrich ourselves only by exchange, in cultural and economic intermixing, in the dialogue between different peoples. For this, we must not indulge in racism or impose our cultural and religious values on others. It must not be said that "Western civilization is superior to other civilizations," nor claimed that the world is experiencing "civilization and culture shock." Cultures travel: they move around and get into homes without even being invited. The only dominant culture is that of intelligence, knowledge, and sharing. In this way culture does not dominate, but opens doors to those seeking to learn and to know what is going on outside their own tribe.

This book is presented in the same spirit as *Racism Explained to My Daughter.** It does not point a finger, it does not teach a moral lesson, but wishes to encourage people to know themselves better. It recalls historical facts, rectifies a few errors, explains a few rituals, defines essential words and concepts, and quashes any excuses for prejudice. The reader will realize, if he or she reads it without distorting glasses, that Islam is a religion like the two other monotheistic religions, that it was the last one revealed, that the prophet Muhammad was the last of the prophets and that he was the continuator of the other prophets who preceded him. Hence, Muslims should ven-

* The New Press, 1999

erate Abraham, Moses, and Jesus just as they venerate Muhammad.

The essense of Islam is in fact in contrast to the obscurantist discourse of the Taliban, of the militants of al-Qa'idah, their leader, Osama bin Laden, and all those barbarians who have used a religion of peace to make war on modernity and the West.

Muhammad Ali became the world heavyweight boxing champion through his talent and thanks to his will and determination. It was not Islam that opened the way to his success. On the other hand, through his faith he strengthened his identity and achieved the serenity and power necessary for living. For him Islam is more than submission to peace, it is a happy acceptance of the peace inside, peace with himself.

Tahar Ben Jelloun
Paris
March 2002

September 11
Explained to Children

My children have not been spared images of the American tragedy of September 11, 2001. The remarks they've heard here and there regarding the terrorists and their belonging to the Arab and Muslim world have worried them.

Thus, one of my children (not quite ten) asked me this questions:

Daddy, am I a Muslim?

Yes, like your parents.

And am I an Arab too?

Yes, you're an Arab even if you don't speak Arabic.

But you saw on TV, the Muslims are bad, they killed a lot of people, I don't want to be a Muslim.

What are you going to do about it?

Starting now I won't turn down pork at the school cafeteria.

If you want, but before giving up being Muslim, I should tell you that the bad men you are talking about are not real Muslims, and there are bad men everywhere.

But people say these men are Arabs. . . .

You must not lump all Arabs together. Not all Arabs are Muslims. There are Christian Arabs in Lebanon, Egypt, Palestine, Sudan. . . .

I saw an old man with a beard who prays like Granddad and then he takes a gun and fires at pictures. Is he a Muslim?

If he prays like Granddad, yes.

Why are these people not real Muslims?

Allah, like the god of the Jews and the Christians, forbids killing yourself, which we call suicide. And He forbids killing other people. So those men who got on airplanes, who killed the pilots with a knife, and then flew the planes into the skyscrapers in New York—those men don't understand the Muslim religion, and they are fanatics.

What's a fanatic?

It's somebody who thinks he's always right and wants to be the most powerful. If you don't agree with him, he becomes very wicked.

America didn't agree with them and that's why they ran the airplane into the skyscraper?

Yes, no one can accept what they did. What they did was horrible.

What did America do to them that they were so cruel?

America, or more exactly the American government, has made many mistakes and been very unfair. They have been bombing the Iraqi people for ten years. Many Iraqi children have died in these bombings. In 1991 the Iraqi army invaded its neighbor Kuwait. America and other countries stepped in and forced the Iraqi army out. Then Iraq was punished by the United Nations. But actually it was the people who were punished, not their leader. It's complicated, you see. It's not as simple as you think, especially because America is a very powerful nation and must take care to be fair. But despite all of that, nothing can justify those mass killings.

But was it Iraqis who attacked America?

No, it was people who say they are Arabs and Muslims. For me, they are crazy people.

But why are they crazy?

Those people were taught when they were kids and attended Koranic school that Allah wanted them to kill the enemies of Islam and then Allah would reward them by sending them to heaven.

I don't get it. You have to kill to go to heaven?

Absolutely not! But they were told to believe that.

And they believed it? Tell me how they were made to believe it.

Their teachers told them the same thing many times over. They gave them examples of soldiers who died in combat, they quoted the Koran that says, "Do not say of those who are killed in God's service that they are dead! No! . . . They are alive. . . ." (Sura II, verse 154). They ended up believing what had been repeated to them thousands of times.

But they are very wicked. They make people die so that they themselves can get to heaven!

It's all lies.

But why do their leaders tell them all this?

Because they're making war on people who do not think the way they do. They do not love life, so they are ready to sacrifice their own provided they take with them as many dead people as possible. They are terrorists.

Daddy, what does "terrorist" mean?

In the word "terrorist" you find the word "terror," that is, a very great fear, a dread, something that makes you tremble and panic. It's horrible.

I don't understand why people who want to go to heaven don't go there by themselves. Why do they kill and terrify the people they don't kill?

I don't know, child. I'm like you, I can't understand how young people who are educated, who have been around in the world, and who have enjoyed the freedom and comfort of America, decide one day to commit mass murder that takes their own lives as well. They do this in the name of Islam. They are doing harm to their own families, to Islam, and to Muslims. It is not their religion that backs them up, for no religion urges the killing of innocent people, and Islam means "submission to peace," not "kill innocent people." So it is a madness that neither you nor I can understand.

When you were a child, did you know that you were a Muslim?

Yes. I was born in a house where I always saw my mother and father saying their prayers.

And you?

I prayed too, but I was lazy, especially in winter when we had to get up early and to wash up in ice-cold water. Because, before any prayer, you have to wash up—that is called ablutions.

So you didn't wash up?

Oh yes, I did, but my father noticed that I did it quickly and superficially and that I didn't like ice-cold water.

What did he say?

One day he called us together, my brother and me, and said this: "My sons, you were born into Islam, and you must obey your parents and God. In principle, you should do the five daily prayers and you should keep the fast of Ramadan. In Islam there is no forcing. No one has the right to force you to do your prayers, neither God nor your father. As the proverb says, On the final Judgment Day, each sheep will be hung by its own hoof. So you are free, I leave you to think about it. The main thing is not to steal, not to lie, not to hit the weak and the sick, not to deceive, not to make he who has nothing feel ashamed, not to mistreat your parents, and above all not to commit injustices. So, my sons, there you have it and the rest is up to you. I have done my duty. It's up to you to be worthy sons."

And then what happened?

I kissed his hand the way I did every morning, and I felt free. I understood that day that I could be a Muslim without practicing the rules and laws of Islam in a disciplined way. I also remember what the principal of the Koranic school told us: "God is merciful!" He repeated, "Praise God the all-merciful"—in other words, God pardons.

But tell me, do you do your prayers or not?

That's a question that shouldn't be asked. We shouldn't answer that kind of question because it involves the person's freedom. If I pray, that's my business alone. If

I pray, it isn't to show people that I am a good Muslim. Some people go to the mosque to be seen, others because they are sincerely carrying out their duties as believers.

Daddy, I'm afraid. I can't sleep.

Don't worry.

I heard there'll be a war.

What war?

I don't know. Even at school, they told us to pay attention: if we see a bag left in a corner, we should call the teacher. I don't know, I'm afraid.

Don't worry, life is good despite everything!

Day 2

I imagined what this discussion would have
been like had I held it with children between
the ages of ten and fifteen.

I anticipated their questions, their worries, and their impatience. Thus, I have under-
taken to explain Islam and Arab civilization to my
children, who were born Muslims, as well as to all children whatever their nationality, their religion, their language, or even their hopes. This is, above all, not a sermon
nor a legal defense. I am not seeking to persuade, but to
describe as objectively and simply as possible the history
of the man who became known as the Prophet, as well as
the history of a religion and a civilization that have provided so much to humanity. I reread the Koran, I con-
sulted books written by specialist, I looked up entries in
The Encyclopedia of Islam, and I have tried to reconstruct in

a few pages fifteen centuries of history in the hope of helping people to understand, if only a little, what is happening today.

Daddy, I haven't understood very well what Islam is. I am a Muslim, but what does that mean?

I am taking this chance to speak to you and to all children who want to know about it. I shall tell you the history of this religion in the form of a story.

Once upon a time, very long ago, more than 1,430 years ago, around the year 570, a little boy was born in Mecca, a town in the Arabian desert. He was called Muhammad. He never saw his father, who died before he was born. He didn't go to school. He grew up without knowing how to read or write. The people there made their living by cattle raising and commerce, which involved caravans that traveled across the country from town to town. Mecca was an important trading center. Caravans came through Mecca from the north, the east, and the south. Not far from there was the town of Jeddah, a port.

What were the people from this region called?

Arabs. They were Bedouins, they traveled in caravans, they were nomads. They lived in tents.

What does "Bedouins" mean?

They were the first inhabitants of Arabia. In the word "Bedouin" we find the Arab word *bada'a,* which means "to appear." The Bedouins were the earliest people. They lived in the desert or the countryside.

And "nomads"?

They are people who move about, who don't have permanent housing. And indeed the Bedouins were small communities that constantly traveled in search of grazing land and water sources. They traveled on the backs of camels.

Little Muhammad was born there. What did his mother do?

Her name was Amina; she, too, died when he was a child, when he was not yet six. So he was an orphan at a very early age. He was raised by a wet nurse, Halima. His grandfather saw to his education. Muhammad grew up in Mecca with his uncles, who were the keepers of the Kaâba, a cubical building containing a famous stone, the Black Stone, on which the prophet Abraham, God's Beloved, had set his foot. It was a sacred stone. Once a year, the Arabs came to Mecca to touch this stone. That is called a pilgrimage. But in this area there were Christians and Jews, that is, Bedouins who believed in a single God. The Jewish religion, which is called Judaism, has existed for 5,762 years; the Christian religion for 2,002 years. At the time, there weren't many such people in this area. The others worshiped statues and stones, which are called idols. There seem to have been 360 idols in Kaâba. Not all the Arabs worshiped idols. Some of them believed in the power of nature, in the power of light, in the force of the wind and in the memory of their ancestors, that is, in those who had gone before them.

What did Muhammad do?

After the earliest years spent with his wet nurse, he lived with his uncle Abou Talib, a poor but very good and upright man. Muhammad considered him a father. From his uncle he learned loyalty, honesty, and goodness. At the age of 25, Muhammad was working for Khadija, a rich widow. She was forty, somewhat older than he. She owned several caravans. He married her, and they had three boys and four girls. Unfortunately, the boys did not survive.

Why did he marry a woman older than himself?

It was his destiny. She was a caravan owner and she entrusted more and more work to the young Muhammad. One day she proposed that he become more than just her employee. He accepted.

Did he remain close to the uncle who had raised him?

Yes. Abou Talib's son, Ali, who was born around 600, was very close to Muhammad; Ali was his cousin, but also his close friend. He was to play an important role upon the death of Muhammad.

How did Muhammad become the head of a religion?

He didn't know beforehand that it would happen. He was a reserved, sensitive man. He must have felt different from other men. He used to go into the mountains in the outskirts of Mecca and withdraw into a cave in order to think about life, nature, and Good and Evil. He meditated.

What does "meditate" mean?

It is thinking deeply, hoping to find a meaning in life. A long time ago, this word meant "caring for a sick person." Muhammad must have been searching in the silence and solitude for a remedy; a remedy for a life in which some people are poor and others rich, some healthy and others sick and weak.

But what could he do for the unfortunate people?

He reflected and sought a way to make them less unhappy. One day, or rather one night, while he was in a cave on Mount Hira, he had a vision, he saw before him a strong, beautiful light; it was a high-ranking angel, who commanded him to read. He said to him, "Read." But Muhammad, who was forty at the time, answered, "I don't know how to read!" Remember, he hadn't gone to school and didn't know how to read or write. The angel, who was named Gabriel, asked Muhammad to repeat after him: "Read in the name of God the creator. He created man, His adherent. Read. For the Lord is very generous; He has taught man by means of the *calame* and taught him what he did not know." Moved and trembling, Muhammad repeated these words after the angel Gabriel.

What does "adherent" mean?

The Arabic word is *alaq,* which means "sticky matter." Some people have translated the word as "blood clot," but actually it refers to a viscous liquid formed by the spermatozoids and called "sperm." Human beings reproduce by means of spermatozoids.

What does "calame" mean?

It is the reed used to make a pencil or pen for writing.

What did he do after this visit? Was he afraid?

He was very worried. Muhammad was a simple man, but he was highly intelligent and was afraid of falling into a trap set by the Devil. Then, returning home, he confided in his wife, Khadija. She went to see Waraka Ibn Nawfal, a learned Christian in Mecca, and asked his opinion and advice about what had just happened. That good and educated man told her that Muhammad was the prophet people were waiting for. God had sent humans a messenger who was to be the last one, a man who would speak to his fellow men and teach them what the brilliant light would dictate to him.

Why does God not speak to men directly?

He preferred to choose a simple, good man in order to pass on his messages to him and entrust him with repeating them to his fellow men. Muhammad, thanks to this brilliant and magnificent light, had this revelation.

What is a revelation?

Something that comes into view and becomes obvious; it is like the truth when we are looking for it, and when it appears, we say, "The truth has been revealed." Muhammad was to announce the word of God. For several years, companions and friends gathered those words and put together a book, the book of the Muslims, the Koran."

What does the word "Koran" mean?

This word comes from the Arabic word *qaraqa,* which means "to read, recite." For 23 years, Muhammad received this book, unique of its kind, sentence by sentence. Later the text was arranged in verses and then in suras, that is, chapters. The angel Gabriel, who appeared in the form of a great dazzling light, was always the means by which God's message reached Muhammad.

What did Gabriel say to Muhammad?

He told him that there was one God, all-powerful and very merciful. He told him that we must be faithful to the word of God, that we must believe in His message, that there is another life after death, that man will be judged by his actions, and that every member of the human race will have to testify about what he has done during his life, that good and just men will be rewarded by going to heaven and that the others, the bad men, the unbelievers, the criminals, will be judged and sent to hell. He told him that we must do good and avoid evil, that men must be well behaved and believers, and that above all we should not worship stones and believe that there are other gods than God.

But our schoolteacher, who is Christian, teaches us the same thing!

You know, as I have told you, that before Muhammad's religion, there were two other religions, Judaism and Christianity. Both of them worship a single God. They, too, had prophets: Moses and Jesus. The Jews, the Christians, and the Muslims were to form "a single community with the believers." Islam came to join these two religions. They are called the monotheistic religions, or the religions of the Book. The book of the Jews is the Torah; the book of the Christians, the Bible; and that of the Muslims, the Koran.

"Mono" . . . I know what that means—only one!

Yes, absolutely. "Monotheist" means "a single God."

So if we have the same God, why are the Muslims and the Jews in the Middle East at war with each other?

You're mixing things up. The Muslims and the Jews are fighting over the same land, but it is not a war of religion. Islam recognizes the prophets of the Jews and the Christians.

How?

The Muslims owe their prophet Muhammad, God's messenger, their worship and love. They owe the same respect to Moses and Jesus. Don't forget that Islam appeared about six centuries after Jesus. Thus it is the most recent monotheistic religion in human history.

What do the Christians think of Muslims?

That would be a long story. But in 1965 at the Vatican in Rome, where the pope lives, there was a meeting of the important people in the Church who recognized that "there were precious values in Islam." This meeting was called the Second Vatican Council.

Explain why what happened to Muhammad was called Islam or the Muslim religion.

The word "Islam" contains the word *salam,* which means "peace." Islam is man's submission to peace, submission to a single God, a God to whom we owe obedience, fidelity, and loyalty.

How can we obey someone we can't see?

When I was little, I was told that God knew everything, heard everything, and saw everything. I asked my mother, "He sees me, He watches even me, little, puny me?" She replied, "Exactly, He is all-powerful. He sees you and if you do something stupid, He'll be displeased." One day I stole a piece of cake and I hid in a trunk to eat it. I told myself, "God will not see me here." I had a bellyache because I'd swallowed the cake without chewing it!

If you're well hidden, God can't see you!

Yes, he can. God can see everything, even what is hidden.

People who are bad, who make war and pray at the same time and say they love God are liars.

God calls them hypocrites. God addressed a whole chapter to Muhammad about hypocrites. He damns them.

Explain the word "hypocrite."

We say that the hypocrite has two faces. He distorts the truth by having you believe that he is telling the truth. A hypocrite is a schemer and a liar.

Day 3

Let's go back to the story of the birth of Islam.

Before we go on, though, what language did the angel speak when the wonderful light surrounded Muhammad?

Arabic.

So God is an Arab!

No, He is not an Arab, not Chinese, not African, not Indian. God is the god of all men without exception. He doesn't distinguish between human beings. That is what His message says.

Then why didn't He speak English, since almost everyone in the world speaks English?

He spoke in the language that was spoken where His messenger Muhammad was. I've told you that Muhammad was living in Arabia and that he spoke Arabic. Because of this, the Arabs consider their language the language of God.

Is that language the same one my grandparents in Morocco speak?

Not completely. In Morocco, they speak an Arabic dialect, in contrast to the Arabic in books, the one known as classical or literary Arabic. But when your grandparents pray, they recite verses from the Koran in classical Arabic.

And what do the Muslims do who aren't Arabs?

They learn the prayers by heart and say them without understanding all the words they are using. In principle, they understand their meaning. The ones who do not speak Arabic read the Koran translated into their own language.

What did Muhammad do so that people believed his story?

His wife understood right away that what he was saying was true. Then came his cousin Ali, who agreed with him and was converted to Islam. After that his best friend Abou Bakr, who was a very respected man, and then his adopted son, Zayd. Then came Bilal, Abou Bakr's black servant. Bilal was a slave. Muhammad set him free and, because he had a very beautiful voice, Muhammad chose him to call people to prayer five times a day. He was Islam's first *muezzin*.

There were slaves?

All societies had slavery. In setting Bilal free, Muhammad set an example so that all those who had slaves would do likewise. Unfortunately, they didn't follow his example.

People didn't agree with him?

No, not everyone. People fought against him even within his own tribe.

He didn't harm anyone, did he?

No, he was a good man, but as the song says, "People don't like someone taking a different road."

He told them to do good and not to betray—

Yes, but you must understand that before the story of this revelation, before Muhammad became a messenger of God, the people of Arabia did what they wanted to do, they didn't have any strict rules to respect; besides, they believed that some stone statues were gods. Muhammad comes and tells them God is Truth, God is Justice, God is Spirit. To live together, you must have a morality, a spirituality; you must worship God, who is not embodied in an object; there are heaven and hell; the things of this world are not important; you must pray five times a day; you must meditate and believe in a God who is very merciful; and so on.

People weren't going to believe him . . .

No, they didn't believe him right away. He was someone who upset their usual ways of doing things. So they struggled against him. In this, God condemns them in a line of the Koran (Sura IX, verse 5): "Kill the idolaters everywhere you find them. Seize them, attack them, lie in ambush for them. But if they repent, if they are strict in their prayers, if they give alms, let them go on their way. In truth, Allah forgives; He is compassionate."

Idolaters are people who do not believe in a single God— right?

They are polytheists and believe in many gods, in stones, in idols made of stone.

What did Muhammad do then?

Muhammad had a very difficult time; in the year 620, he lost his wife as well as his adoptive father, his uncle Abou Talib. He found himself alone to struggle against the people of his tribe who sought to kill him. He left Mecca with Ali and Abou Bakr. They took shelter in a cave to escape the armed men who were after them intending to kill them. In Islam, there are no miracles as in the two other religions, but people tell the story that the entrance to this cave was sealed by a spider web that protected Muhammad and his two companions.

Now I know why you've told me not to kill spiders! They are sacred animals!

In any case, thanks to this web, the Prophet was saved. Later he left for another town, Medina, where he was safe. The Muslim era begins on this date, 622. It is called year 1 of the Hegira. Now we are in the year 1422 of the Hegira.

What does "Hegira" mean?

The word comes from the term *hajara,* which means "to emigrate," that is, leave for another town or country.

So Muhammad was an émigré!

Yes. He was forced to flee to go on receiving and spreading God's message. The Muslim era began. The calendar follows the phases of the moon. That is why we never know ahead of time the exact date of the start of the month. Starting in Medina, Islam gradually became organized and established its five precepts known as the Five Pillars of Islam. "Pillar" means "a support that holds up a building."

What are "precepts"?

Rules, commandments, orders.

So what are the rules of the Muslims?

There are five of them, and when they are respected, they make a true Muslim of you. The first rule is *chachada,* affirmation of the faith—that is, that you must accept in the depths of your soul the idea that there is only one God, Allah, and that Muhammad is His messenger. You must utter this sentence, the one that every Muslim says at the moment of his death. We say he is testifying. He raises the index finger of his right hand and says, "I attest that the only God is Allah, and that Muhammad is His messenger."

Can you say that in Arabic?

Ach hadou anna lâ Illaha illa Allah wa anna Muhammad Rassoul Allah.

Can you say the same thing when you are not dying?

Of course.

Do you say it often?

Sometimes I do.

How can you be sure it's true?

That is what we call faith—that is, you are certain, it is obvious. No one can manage to prove to you the opposite of what you believe. For Muslims, we have to say it and above all not doubt it.

Must it be said in Arabic or in any language?

What does the language matter? What matters is that you be convinced of these words.

Suppose I'm not convinced. Then what happens?

Then you're not a Muslim. That's all.

And the second rule?

The prayers. There are five of them a day. The first of them is at sunrise. The second one is when the sun is at its zenith. The third one is in the middle of the afternoon. The fourth is at sunset. And the last one is at night. All these prayers are made facing Mecca.

Do you have to go pray when the call to prayer begins?

Yes, in principle. If you're working or sick, you can pray later on. If you are handicapped, you can pray mentally.

Earlier you spoke of "ablutions." Can you explain how and why they are done?

When we pray, we are speaking to God, so we are supposed to be clean. The ablutions are the washing up we do just before praying. There are two kinds of ablutions: the complete ablutions, which consist in washing every part of the body after having sexual relations, and the simple ablutions, which consist in washing one's face, forearms, hands, and feet.

If you wash up five times a day, you must be the champion of cleanliness!

You're right. Muhammad said that good hygiene comes from faith.

What do the prayers say?

We glorify God and his prophet. We recite the first sura of the Koran.

The one where the angel says to Muhammad, "Read"?

No. The Koran is not written in the order in which the verses were revealed. The Koran begins with a short sura called the *Fatiha,* the opening. In each prayer, we celebrate and glorify not only the prophet Muhammad, but also the other prophets: Abraham, Moses, and Jesus. In Arabic, we call them Ibrahim, Moussa, and Issa.

The third pillar?

It is the fast during the month of *Ramadan.* The Muslim must abstain from eating and drinking from sunrise to sunset for a month. He is thus doing an apprenticeship of hunger and a test of his will to resist temptations and of his ability to meditate about life and what lies beyond it. It is the month in which he must dedicate himself to contemplation, to prayer, and to an examination of his behavior in life. The end of Ramadan is marked by a festival called *Aïd Seghir.*

Must everyone stop eating and drinking?

No. Children who have not yet reached the age of puberty and persons who are ill must not do the fasting. Nor women during their periods.

The other pillars?

The alms, called *zakat*. It is a share of the money the believer has earned during the year; he gives it to the poor, the needy, and this must be done unobtrusively. We must not brag about it or point to the poor in order to humiliate them. We must help people who are in need.

The other rule or precept is the pilgrimage to Mecca, called *al-Hajj*. (Those who can't afford it or are handicapped are excused.) The Muslim travels to Mecca and Medina to meditate at the Prophet's grave and walk around the temple, the Kaâba, attempting to touch the famous Black Stone. The pilgrimage takes place every year at the time of the *Aïd al-Adha,* better known by the name "sheep festival." The festival celebrates the sacrifice of Abraham, the Beloved of God, he who almost sacrificed his son; God sent him a sheep, whose throat he slit instead of his son's. It's a very popular festival. For many people, it's a chance to eat meat.

Isn't it also a rule not to eat pork?

Islam says that we must not eat pork because pigs feed on all the garbage thrown into the trash.

But today pigs are raised in a clean way like sheep.

Yes, but it's very hard to change a religious law. The other prohibition concerns alcohol. There are three verses, revealed at different times, forbidding the consumption of fermented beverages. The man who gets drunk loses self-control. But Islam insists on self-mastery and also on man's freedom, which makes him responsible.

Isn't drinking being free?

Freedom consists in giving the human being choice. Man can drink or abstain from drinking. If he drinks and becomes drunk, he is the one responsible for what he does.

Are other things forbidden?

Yes, gambling for money, and earning interest with money. These prohibitions are less well observed. People consider them less serious than the other prohibitions. We must add to these prohibitions that a Muslim woman does not have the right to marry a non-Muslim, unless the man she marries converts to Islam.

But the men have to right to marry non-Muslim women, I suppose!

Yes, they have the right to marry non-Muslim women.

That's not fair.

It is because of the family name, which is passed on through the father. This is a society in which the patriarch—that is, the male head of the family—dominates. It is called a patriarchal society. Accordingly, women are submissive, dependent on men, and thus able to be influenced. If a woman marries a non-Muslim, she runs the risk of being lost to Islam, and her children also risk being raised in the father's religion.

Day 4

It was in Medina, where Muhammad sought
refuge, where he felt safe, that he planned his
battle for the maximum number of people
possible to become Muslims so that there
would be a close-knit community of people gathered in their faith in a single God. Muhammad fought
against all the tribes that threatened the Muslims, and
acted so that even his enemies in the end converted to
Islam, such as Abou Soufyan, the head of one of the tribes
that had fought him. According to the reports of wit-
nesses, Muhammad appeared to be a man of action, a military and political leader. There were two major battles:
Badr and Ohod. With him was born the idea of *Oumma is-
lamiya*. The Oumma is the community, the group of all
Muslims. In the year 632, Muhammad traveled to Mecca
to carry out the pilgrimage to the Kaâba. It is said that on

leaving, he turned toward the Kaâba and said, "How beautiful this temple is! Nothing is greater and more beautiful than man's dignity!"

What is "dignity"?

It is self-respect, the sense of being faithful to the values and qualities that make one proud to be a man. Its opposite, the lack of dignity, is baseness, the absence of any value; it means giving up on being a just and courageous man. The prophet put dignity above the beauty of the Kaâba. That shows the importance he gave to this quality that every human being should possess.

What happened next?

He sensed that God was going to call him back and that his mission was finished. He set off for Medina, where he died on June 8, 632.

Who took his place?

No one. He was a prophet, God's last messenger on earth. God sent him to men, and then recalled him. His friend and companion Abou Bakr led the prayer in the name of all the Muslims. He was elected by some of the population as "caliph," that is, leader of the Muslims who follow the rules left by Muhammad. These are the Muslims called *Sunnis*. Others preferred Ali, Muhammad's cousin. These are called *Shiites*. They opposed the Sunnis when Ali wanted to become caliph. Today the Shiites represent about 10 percent of the world's Muslims. They distinguish themselves from the Sunnis by having representatives called "mullahs."

On television I've seen Muslims striking their chests—is that common?

Those are Shiites. They express their punishment by hurting themselves.

What punishment?

When their leader, Hussein, one of Ali's sons, was killed on October 10, 680, in the battle of Karbala, the Shiites felt guilty for not having protected and saved him. That is the reason that every year they celebrate this date by mourning. Some of them carry this to extremes by punishing themselves and violently hitting themselves sometimes to the point of bleeding.

Starting at that time, Islam was to spread throughout that region and beyond. Twenty years after Muhammad's death, Othman, the third caliph, assembled the 114 chapters (suras) that make up the Koran, the sacred book, the holy book and divine word.

Have you read the Koran?

When I was your age and even before going to elementary school, I went for two years to the Koranic school, where they taught us to learn the Koran by heart. Even though I didn't know how to read yet, I learned the verses one after another. The next day I recited them; if I made a mistake, I was hit with a rod.

And your parents didn't say anything?

They didn't know about it. Every evening I made an effort to memorize the verses to recite the next day.

Did you understand everything you learned by heart?

Not at all. I knew that you had to worship Allah, the only God, that you had to do good, not lie, not steal, obey your parents, respect the schoolteacher, pray, or else God would punish you. Sometimes I was afraid, especially when God spoke of hell and Judgment Day. But right after, there were verses that reminded us that God is forgiving and pardons those who have gone astray.

What scared you the most?

When the teacher at the Koranic school described what awaited a man who kills himself, who commits suicide, that is, who defies the divine will. You know, someone who kills himself by burning will repeat this act eternally in hell. Anyone who throws himself from a building will throw himself for infinity. It is horrible! This is true if one is a believer.

So, to talk about what is happening now, God will punish the people who killed the Americans?

I think so.

Why, aren't you sure? If not, everything you've told me wouldn't be true.

Everything I've told you is true—it is part of the history of humanity. A man sometimes asks himself questions about God, especially when he sees the suffering, injustice, and poverty that prevail in the world. The Christians say "God is love." The Muslims say "God is justice, God is truth." So when the world is racked with wars, when young people give up on living, sacrificing themselves while killing innocent people in the name of Islam, then men ask themselves questions. It is only animals that don't doubt.

What does "doubt" mean?

Religious faith is a belief. To believe is to accept, to trust in the doctrine and to remain faithful to it. Religions don't put up with doubt or scoffing. Doubt is the act of not believing blindly —of using reason in matters of belief. To doubt is to ask questions and hope for the right answers. So logic and belief don't go together.

And are you a believer?

When you think logically, it isn't as easy to be a believer as the people with faith think. Let me say, to answer your question, that I believe there is spirituality, something that is both mysterious and beautiful that overawes me. We can call it God. I feel very tiny in the face of the immensity of the universe, and I am not able to understand everything. As one philosopher has said, "Intelligence is the incomprehension of the world."

I don't understand.

You should distrust people who claim to have the answers for all questions. Fanatics say that religion can answer all the questions in the world. That's impossible.

And Islam?

You know that this religion has given the world a beautiful civilization, a very great culture. What is specific to Islam is that there are no priests, bishops, or popes. There are no intermediaries between the believer and God.

I know that among the Catholics the priests don't have the right to get married!

Yes. I found it odd that on Sunday my friends in high school went to church to confess to a priest. I told them, "But you ought to talk with God, He is the one from whom you should ask forgiveness if you have done some-thing wrong." They told me that that was their tradition.

So there is no confession in Islam.

No.

Before Islamic civilization was insulted, as it now is, by people who are crazed or ignorant, it was for three hun-dred years, between the ninth and the eleventh centuries, at the height of progress and culture in the world.

Day 5

To tell you about the magnificent era called the Golden Age of the Arabs, before speaking about the current situation, which is, as you said, particularly bad for the Arab and Muslim countries, I shall ask you to imagine a dream, to enter a marvelous world where peace, wisdom, and harmony between persons prevail, where there is curiosity about everything that is different, a world where children are happy to go to school because there they not only memorize verses of the Koran but are soon introduced to foreign languages, music, and even science.

I'll close my eyes and follow along with your tale.

The Muslim religion encouraged the Arabs to spread Allah's message throughout the world. They went to the

Middle East (Syria, Egypt, and Iraq, known as the Fertile Crescent), to Persia, and to North Africa. These victories were not always peaceful. There were battles, resistance, and deaths. That was understandable, for the Arab armies occupied some countries without the acquiescence of their people. These armies often camped near oases and rivers, where they prepared new expeditions. There were also conflicts within the Muslim clans. Gradually, thanks to the spreading of Islam, the Arabs were to have their own empire. The Arab culture was to grow and become enriched because it knew how to open itself up to the world. The language of the Koran was to replace Greek and Persian to the point that a tenth-century Iranian historian said, "The Arabic language is the repository of all the arts of the earth; it enters deeply into our hearts, its power casts a spell in the most secret part of our beings."

What does "repository" mean?

In this expression, it means that the Arabic language contains all the arts, that it gives birth to works of art such as poetry, the sciences, medicine, and so on. Everything that leads humanity to develop and that makes it better.

Then, everyone spoke Arabic!

No, not in every country, but at that time, the Arabic language had become as important as Greek in the history of antiquity.

I don't know the importance of Greek in ancient times, but I suppose that Arabic was taught in all the schools, not the way it is today.

Everyone learned Arabic because the Arab Muslim learned men took up the huge task of translating everything important that had been produced in other languages. Thus they translated books of Greek philosophy and works in Persian and Indian languages."

Explain the word "philosophy."

It is the love of wisdom and learning. In philosophy we learn to think while studying what the ancients already discovered and wrote. It is using reason to think methodically and to know where one's life is headed.

Good. Let's say I understood!

To pursue the point, philosophy is the study of what we think. This is the reason that when the Arabs translated and published the philosophical works of the Greeks, they were doing a great service to humanity. It was thanks to the Arabs that people discovered the great Greek philosophers. The Arabic language became the leading language everywhere. Science, medicine, mathematics, geography, astronomy—all these were taught in Arabic. The prophet Muhammad himself, who hadn't had a chance to go to school, said that every Muslim should go in search of science all over the world.

When the Muslims occupied a country, were the people forced to learn Arabic?

They were not forced to, but if they wanted to go very far in their studies, to learn a lot, they had to know Arabic. The language of Islam stood out as the leading spoken and written language in the world. Beginning in the ninth century, the language of science from Spain to China was Arabic. Scientific research, which makes new discoveries possible, was done in Arabic, whether in Baghdad, Damascus, Cairo or Grenada, Palermo or Samarkand. Everywhere people built universities and libraries called Houses of Wisdom.

What is a "House of Wisdom"?

It was a center where people gathered who wanted to dig deeper into their studies and to talk with people who were more experienced and better educated than they were, a place where everything was done to make the acquisition of knowledge easier.

And people went there?

Yes, there was a hunger for knowledge, a passion for studying. The people discovered the world, various cultures, various languages.

Who encouraged the translations and the studies?

The caliphs; that is, the leaders of the countries, those who were spreading Islam. But rich people, too, gave money for translating the important works and for building Houses of Wisdom, that is, houses of culture.

If everyone spoke Arabic, did the Europeans do so as well?

No. The Europeans benefited from the Arab discoveries and translations to make progress in their own culture.

What was the capital of this Arab empire?

It was Baghdad, the largest city in Iraq. The most famous caliph was named Harun al-Rashid, the one talked about in *A Thousand and One Nights.* He lived during the first part of the ninth century. It was from Baghdad that scholars and students left for other countries in search of manuscripts in science, medicine, or philosophy to be translated into Arabic.

But did the Arabs only translate books?

No, they wrote, did research in the sciences, in medicine for example; they built universities, *madrasahs,* that is, religious schools, libraries, mosques, palaces, and so on. The work of translation means that the Arabs did not consider themselves scholars who had nothing more to learn. On the contrary, the truly cultured person is the one who says that we can always learn from others. They wanted to know what people who were neither Muslim nor Arab were thinking and what they were doing in the fields of science and letters, architecture, commerce—

Explain how people translate.

To go from one language to another is not easy. It's a matter of transmitting the equivalent of what is written in one language to another language. Translation is often the sign of a curious mind. I'll give you an example: even today, the Arabs go on translating the works of writers from Europe, the United States, and Latin America. In Arab bookstores you find as many if not more books translated from foreign languages than books written directly in Arabic. The Arabs have a hunger for learning. If you go into an American bookstore, for example, you will notice that there are very few translated books. A recent study revealed that for every hundred books brought out by American publishers, only three were translations. What other people have written or thought doesn't really interest them!

They are tough!

Mainly they are rich and think they don't need the culture of other people.

Go on telling me about the time when the Arabs were strong.

Their strength was not physical. They had understood that the true conquest is done not with weapons but with culture, even if they were at war with other peoples.

Define the word "culture" for me.

I'm tempted to say it's everything that makes us different from animals. Culture comes from the word "to cultivate," that is, to plow the earth and plant seeds in it. Human beings need to eat and drink and to be in good health. But they have just as great a need to learn about the world they live in. Culture is the product of intelligence, which makes it possible for us to develop our minds, to think better, and to make contact with what our ancestors have left us. Culture is passed down from generation to generation. The whole of its expressions and developments are called "civilization."

What did our ancestors leave us?

That question lets me go back and talk about the era of great Arab intellectuals. The Arabs left—not just to us other Arabs and Muslims but to all humanity—many fine things: algebra (this is an Arab word meaning "reduction") and the zero—yes, the numeral 0. You may say that's nothing, but it is the very basis of all mathematics.

In Arabic, zero is pronounced *cifr,* which means "empty," and gave us the word "cipher," meaning "number." Without going into historical details, let me just tell you that the person who most encouraged the scholars, poets, and researchers was named al-Ma'amun, the son of Harun al-Rashid. He ruled over an immense empire whose capital was Baghdad, which at the time—in the ninth century—had more than a million inhabitants, who practiced various religions. At that time, Rome, the largest city in Europe, had only 30,000 people. Meetings took place between scholars from India, China, Europe, and the Arab world. Baghdad was the cultural capital of the world. Thus, every Tuesday the caliph invited scholars and men of culture in Baghdad to spend the day discussing, reflecting, and exchanging ideas and opinions. The Houses of Wisdom multiplied. It should be added that paper, imported from China, made possible more and more work for copyists.

Weren't books printed?

No. Printing wasn't invented until much later, in the fifteenth century (the person who made the first attempts at printing was Gutenberg, who was born in Mainz around 1400). The first paper mill was built in Baghdad in 794. Other paper-manufacturing plants were built in Egypt, Palestine, and Syria. Along with the Chinese, the Arabs of Sicily and of Andalusia were to introduce the paper industry to Europe.

Day 6

Today I will tell you about the Arab and Muslim presence in Andalusia, in southern Spain. Historians tell us that, when the Arabs arrived in Andalusia, they were shocked by the country's cultural impoverishment despite the cultural legacy of the Roman Empire. One historian even wrote, "It was a complete vacuum. Hordes of immigrants arriving from Arabia and Syria found people unable to provide them with anything whatever. There was nothing for them to adopt, assimilate, imitate, or develop." At the same time as Baghdad, Córdoba was to become the most important cultural center of the Muslim world. The caliph Abd al-Rahman III ruled over Muslim Spain for half a century. He made a magnificent city of Córdoba, a city radiant with culture. He surrounded himself with Muslim, Jewish, and Christian scholars, and provided them with the financial backing to carry on their researches. It was the era in which Andalusian poetry—a wonderful symbol of the Judaic-Muslim encounter—the literature of love, developed to the point where it had a profound and lasting influence in the West. In "Elsa's Madman," the French poet Louis Aragon tells of all he owed to the Arab poetry of the time.

Can you explain what he owed?

It is a lyrical love poetry that sings and weeps of love. Louis Aragon, the great twentieth-century poet, was much inspired by these songs in writing his long love poem to his wife, Elsa. And then there is the very beautiful mystical poetry.

What does "mystical" mean.

There is "mystery" in this word. The mystical is that which has a strong internal relationship with God and excludes any other connection; this relationship is like faith and can't be easily explained. Mystical poetry is the celebration of an immense love of God. In the Muslim world, the mystics are called Sufis. The word comes from the Arabic word *sof,* which means "wool." The Sufis wore clothing woven of coarse wool, thus distinguishing themselves from people who wore luxurious, brightly colored clothes. The Sufi gave up the superficial things of life to devote himself entirely to prayer, meditation, and the love of God.

Were they poets?

Yes. Poets have also left their impact on the Muslim civilization. The most famous one was al-Hallaj. He said, "I am He whom I love," speaking of God. One day he went into the streets of Baghdad and said, "I am the Truth." This confusion of himself with God was not tolerated, and he was considered a man possessed. In 922 he was arrested, judged, and condemned to death. He left poems of great beauty. You should also know that God distrusts poets. In Sura XXVI, verse 224, it is said, "As for poets, only lost souls follow them," that is, people who have gone astray, those who have taken the wrong way. It also says there, "What they say, they do not do."

But you once told me that what you love most in the Koran is the poetry!

The Koran is written in a very beautiful language. I find it full of poetry. But the term "poets" in verse 224 is meant to apply to those who concern themselves only with words and not actions. It is not what defines poets in general.

So everything that was good was Arab!

Let's say the Arabs had understood something simple: to advance, to enrich yourself, your should not close up your house, but open the doors and the barriers, go out toward others, take an interest in what they have written and in what they have built. The Arabs wanted to advance, and for that they needed to learn what the ancients of other countries had already done. The intelligence of the Arabs lay in being modest and accepting the fact that the scholar is someone who begins by saying, "I know nothing." They went looking for science where it had been developed by others, in Greece for example.

Why Greece?

Because greater Greece of the third and fourth centuries B.C., that is, 2,400 years ago, was the place where scholars worked in mathematics, astronomy, medicine, and philosophy.

Did all this happen in Greece?

No, it also went on in Persia, now called Iran.

What is astronomy?

The study of the stars and their positions in the sky.

Were the Arabs also interested in the sky?

Obviously, for to get your bearings on the ocean, you have to know the position of the stars in the sky. Did you know that the first two celestial observatories were built in 827, one in Damascus, the other in Baghdad?

But didn't the Greeks study the stars?

Yes, in the second century A.D., there was Ptolemy, a great astronomer. The Arabs read what he had written and continued his research. The one most inspired by Ptolemy was named Ibu Al Haytham (who died in 1040). He was a mathematician, physicist, and astronomer. He wrote a 1,000-page treatise on optics that was, from the thirteenth to the sixteenth century, the basis in the Eastern world for orientation on land and sea.

What is optics about?

Everything concerning the eye, vision, and the technical means for observing those things that can't be seen by the naked eye.

The Arabs were strong in everything!

Once again I insist: their strength came from their humility. They accepted learning and didn't tell themselves they were wise men, nor that their civilization was better than any other.

What is humility?

It is being modest. Not thinking that we know everything and that no one has anything to teach us. Humility is, as they say in Morocco, "having a small head," the opposite of a swelled head. The wise man begins by recognizing that he doesn't know a lot and has a great deal to learn.

You've told me that, in some Arab countries, they call the doctor the wise man, al-hakim.

Yes, indeed. Arab medicine was the work of great learned men and consequently wise men. The oldest of the known hospitals was built by Harun al-Rashid around 800. Two great names stand out in the history of medicine: al-Razi, who was from Iran, and Avicenna, who was born in the steppes of central Asia. The latter wrote in Arabic the *Canon of Medicine,* a five-volume encyclopedia recognized in the West as "the peak and masterpiece of Arab science." It was translated into Latin in the twelfth century. It dominated the teaching of medicine in Europe up to the end of the seventeeth century. Here is its definition of medicine: "Medicine is the science that studies the human body, either healthy or ill, for the purpose of preserving health when that already exists and reestablishing it when it is lacking."

In the same era, a doctor, al-Zahraoui, made progress in the science of surgery and surgical instruments. In Europe surgery didn't exist until the thirteenth century. It came late because the Christian religion did not approve of this science. Today, Muslims are accused of being behind the times, but the Christians also took the same path.

Right now, it's hard to be a Muslim!

Why do you say that?

I'm not the one who says it. I heard it on TV.

It's true that because of a few fanatics who claim that they are Islamic, the Muslims are poorly understood and badly thought of right now. But, before coming back to it, let me give you some examples of Muslims who were ahead of the rest of the world.

In what field?

In literature, for example. You know the fables of La Fontaine?

Yes, of course.

Well, a long time before La Fontaine, an Arab writer, Ibn al-Muqaffa (eighth century) translated and adapted into Arabic Indian stories under the title *Kalila and Dimna.* La Fontaine read the French translation first published in 1644. He was inspired by these tales and those of Aesop to write his own animal stories.

La Fontaine was a copier!

No, not a copier, but an intelligent man who could take what there was to take and write for the children of

France. But without Ibn al-Muqaffa, there would probably not be La Fontaine's *Fables*.

Another example!

You know the story of Robinson Crusoe?

Yes, we read it in school.

In the twelfth century, a man who lived in Grenada and then in Tangier and Marrakech, wrote *Hay Ibn Yaqdan*. It is the story of a man alone on a desert island who discovers on his own the great truths of life that lead him to what he calls "the light of God." A prophet from an island nearby confirms for him that the truths revealed by religion are the very ones that he had been able to discover on his own. This work preceded Daniel Defoe's book by some five centuries.

Another example!

Marco Polo is renowned for having traveled around the world. Well, before him, an Arab, Ibn Batouta, who was born in 1304 in Tangier, went around the world twice. He left a diary in which he tells what he saw and heard.

What else?

Flavio Gioja, an Italian from Amalfi, is often considered the inventor of the compass. In fact, it was because of some Arab sailors that he discovered this instrument that makes it possible to get one's bearing on land and sea. The commercial Arab merchantmen were the masters of the seas as early as the twelfth century. It wasn't until 1302 that Flavio Gioja was to discover in a book the existence of this instrument invented by the Arabs.

Okay! The Arabs invented many things. And today, are they no longer inventors?

To give you an idea of the current state of things in the Arab and Muslim countries, I need to tell you a bit more history. As I was saying, Islam led Arabs all over the world to spread the Prophet's message and also to convert as many people as possible to this new religion. In leaving home, they discovered another world and they wanted to educate themselves and take part in the development of humanity. That was what happened. There were battles, deaths, and conflicts within Islam itself. When the Muslims occupied a country, they took the Christians and the Jews under their protection. These people owed them a tax.

They were buying their protection?

Yes, as minorities.

Minorities?

On Islamic territory, the Jews and the Christians, whom the Muslims called "the people of the Book"—that is, people whose religion is based on a sacred book, as the Koran is for the Muslim—were not very numerous, and that is what is called a minority. Because of this situation, they had to put a certain amount of money directly into the treasury in exchange for a guarantee of physical and social safety.

Why did they have to pay in order to live with the Muslims?

It may be that the Muslims were trying to get them to convert to Islam. But this situation did not last for too long a time. Despite this, between the ninth and eleventh centuries, it was intelligence, knowledge, and culture that characterized the Muslims' actions. After Avicenna (980–1037), who was studied in Europe up until the seventeenth century, and after al-Farabi, who drew up a general table of the sciences, came Averroës. He was an important man.

More than the others?

Yes, because he went even further than his predecessors. He came a century after Avicenna. Born in 1126 in Córdoba, he died in exile in Morocco in 1198.

Why was he exiled to Morocco?

Actually, because he was a philosopher. It was he who recorded the legacy of the Greek philosopher Aristotle and made it available to the West. He was also a great Muslim jurist.

What does "jurist" mean?

Someone who studies the law, that is, the rules and the laws that are the basis of every society and that define justice.

Good. So he was in favor of wisdom and justice.

He tried to introduce reason into the faith.

Reason is logic, and faith is belief, no?

Yes, he attempted to give a certain logic to the fact of believing. Then, too, he observed that the Muslim religion is used by people who have other objectives. There were some sects, groups that refused to discuss their principles and particularly to accept contributions from foreigners. There were disputes. The house of Islam was no longer the House of Wisdom. Averroës condemned all this, but the politicians in Córdoba had a different opinion. He fled and sought protection in Morocco. Starting at this time, the Muslim civilization was to be contaminated by fanaticism and intolerance. But these were not the only signs to explain its decadence. It was also the whole period of the Crusades.

Day 7

What does "decadence" mean?

A period of decline, when something gets worse and, instead of making progress, goes downhill. A house that is not kept up, that is vacant or mistreated, deteriorates; it goes to pieces, nothing works inside. A civilization is like a large house. If its foundation is solid, its walls made of good stone, and if the people living there bring in new resources and provide beautiful things, the house will remain in good shape. Well, it's more complicated than that, but a civilization is composed of its heritage, what its ancestors have left it as a legacy. You have to know how to take care of a civilization just as you would a beautiful old house.

Hasn't the Arab civilization been well kept up?

After its time of glory and light, it took some hard blows, first because divisions developed within the great house, rivalries among the caliphs. These leaders had a greater and greater lust for power; they were not thinking of the general interest but of their immediate selfish interests. Furthermore the caliphates of Baghdad and Córdoba were Sunnis, that is, in the classic tradition of the Prophet, whereas the Fatimid caliphate in Cairo was Shiite, that is, a supporter of Ali.

What form did these divisions take?

Starting in 1055, the caliphs brought in Seldjoukid mercenaries (from present-day Turkey) to defend their territory. For example, this Seldjoukid army stopped the Christians from reaching Jerusalem's holy places and persecuted them. In this way they gained political power.

Then what happened?

From 1096 to 1099, Pope Urban II took advantage of these Arab divisions and the mercenaries to launch the Crusades against the Muslims. At the start, he was responding to an appeal for help from the Byzantine emperor, whose capital, Constantinople, was threatened by the Seldjoukid Muslims. Later, the Christian armies went on their own conquests.

Where does the word "crusade" come from?

From the word "cross," since the cross is the symbol of the Christians because Jesus was crucified. The Crusades made war in the name of Christianity against those who were opposed to that religion or stood in the way of its expansion. At the time, Islam was still spreading and doing well in every way. Altogether there were eight expeditions by Christian armies. The last one occurred in 1223. The Catholic princes took Córdoba in 1236, then Seville in 1248. These were political and military defeats for the Arab and Muslim civilization. Only Grenada was able to resist. It was to be the last home of the Arab civilization in Europe. It fell into the hands of the Catholic kings in 1492. It was the end of an era and of a great civilization. The world changed. That was also the year that Christopher Columbus discovered America.

What happened then to the Arabs of Andalusia?

There were Jews and Muslims there. They were driven out, deported from Spain. Those who wanted to stay were told, You can choose between two things, baptism or death.

What did that mean?

Either become a Christian or die. Many of them chose to convert to Catholicism. But, despite this conversion, they were still persecuted, because in their hearts they hadn't given up their faith. They were called Marranos. They were persecuted and deported in great numbers from Spain. This is called the Inquisition. It ended on September 22, 1609. Eventually, Catholic Spain was to absorb, without ever acknowledging it, everything that the Arabs had brought to this region.

Among the Muslims who had to flee Grenada during the reconquest of this area by the Catholics, there was a scholar, a geographer, Leon the African. Under his real name, Hassan Al Wazzan (the Weigher), he spent several years in Rome in the service of Pope Leon X (1518). He taught Arabic and Italian and introduced to the pope's court Greek texts translated into Arabic, which he later translated into Latin. He is a symbol of understanding between East and West.

What became of the Muslims and Arabs?

The Arab world was isolated; trade with Europe was forbidden; Arab philosophy continued to be taught in the European universities, but it ceased to make progress or to be studied in the Arab and Muslim world.

What was studied instead?

Instead of philosophy, which teaches us method, doubt, and reflection, which opens up for us many new horizons about the thought of other societies, people taught the Islamic religion and nothing but the Islamic religion. Now, "religion" means "belief," and hence the absence of reflection and doubt. So people went from a tradition of openness to the world to isolation, a closing in on oneself. It was an impoverishment. This was to be very serious for the Muslim and Arab world. It took time, but we now see the result. When a people have been conquered, they suffer the consequences of defeat for a very, very long time.

What happened between the sixteenth century and the present?

Many things. But let us try to understand why the Arab world underwent a long period of decline.

What does "decline" mean?

To decline means to go down in level and quality. We say of someone who is ill that his health has declined; or, if his sight is poor, that his vision has declined; if he doesn't hear well, then his hearing has declined. It is like decadence. There is the sign of a slow falling off.

Why, then, was there this decline in the Arab world?

The acquisition of knowledge, the translations, the meetings among scholars, philosophical freedom—all this had been desired, financed, and protected by the princes. This openness met a need to understand the world in order to govern a vast empire where there were not only Arab peoples. The day when the princes started fighting among themselves, the scholars and philosophers found no means of political or financial support to get on with their work.

Tell me the name of an outstanding Arab scholar of this time.

If you can keep only one name in mind, the last great Arab scholar, one who wrote a book of universal import, was Ibn-Khaldūn. He was the inventor of what today is called sociology, that is, the study of society's structure and behavior. He lived in North Africa at the end of the fourteenth century and the beginning of the fifteenth (1332–1406). He studied the Arabs' social behavior and ways of thinking. He observed them carefully and had many criticisms. He opened the way for criticism and change. He warned the caliphs against the unqualified persons in charge of religious instruction who took advantage of it to mislead the people. He was against certain people using the mosques for teaching things other than the Koran. Even way back then, he saw the dangers of using Islam for reasons that had nothing to do with religion. He was a visionary. He showed the influence that climate can have on people's moods and ways of thinking. We had to wait for the end of the nineteenth century and the beginning of the twentieth for minds as intelligent and open as Ibn-Khaldūn's was to propose reforms to Islam.

What are "reforms"?

Certain changes of rules and habits in practicing religion.

Is it possible to change something in the Muslim religion?

It is not a matter of changing the values and precepts on which it is based, but rather, while sticking to what is fundamental to it, of introducing reforms into it. This takes courage and perseverance. Among the names to remember are the Afghan Jamal Eddine al-Afghan (who died in 1897) and the Egyptian Muhammad Abduh (who died in 1905). They advocated dialogue, tolerance, and particularly adaptation to the modern world. They said that we should not blindly accept what the ancient teachers laid down as rules for Islamic conduct, that the time when Islam was born was very different from modern times. The rules for changing things in the Muslim countries are based on a verse of the Koran that says, "God does not change the condition of a people as long as the people do not change what it is in itself" (Sura XIII, verse 11). This means that if the Muslims are now thought poorly of in the world, it may not be the fault of others, of the non-Muslims. It is up to the Muslims to change what is bad or ill in their own society. Even if non-Muslims have wronged Islamic peoples, they should not be blamed for everything that's going badly in Muslim countries. Each person has his share of the responsibility. The Crusades are a distant memory, along with colonization. Though some young Muslims have become violent fanatics, the reason is that their education was poor and they were left in the hands of ignorant people without scruples. There was a lack of knowledge or of will to make these young Muslims love development, culture, and life. Poverty and illiteracy were allowed to spread. There was a fear of freedom, and nothing was done against corruption and injustice. These young Muslims turned to a religion that they did not understand well. They have strayed, as the Koran says. They are in error. The root of evil is not always in other people.

What are "scruples"?

You know what name we give to the little pebble that gets into your shoe and bothers you when you walk?

No. An annoying pebble?

It's called "scruple" because it is the grain of sand that prevents the good man from sleeping. He is bothered by something that can be a law, a rule, or a principle. Unscrupulous people sleep with no worries. They are not bothered by the lack of respect for principles.

Day 8

What was happening in the Arab world when it began a period of decline?

From the Arab and Muslim Empire came the Ottoman, that is Turkish, Empire. The Turks set themselves up in Egypt, Lebanon, Syria, Iran, the Balkans, Tunisia, and Algeria. Morocco resisted and so escaped their grip. The height of the Ottoman military power was the sixteenth century. The state religion was Islam. The great empire went through a decline in the nineteenth century. After the First World War, Turkey chose to become a modern state, separating politics from religion. The caliphate, that is, the spiritual and political leadership of all the Muslims, was eliminated in 1922. Thanks to Kemal Atatürk, Turkey became a secular state.

What is "secular"?

To be secular is to be nonreligious.

Does that mean not believing in God?

No, one can believe in God and still be secular. However, in a secular state, religion cannot be used to impose laws on people's lives. Secularism became official in France starting on December 9, 1905, the date when the separation of church and state became official. An example: in French public schools, the clergy do not have the right to teach. They can, on the other hand, have their own schools. There are churches, synagogues, and mosques. Each person has the right to pray where he wants to. The state does not get involved in the practice of religion. Turkey was the first Muslim country to become a secular state.

Is that important?

Given what's happening right now, it's very important to separate religion and politics. As long as a barrier is not set up between the two, there'll be problems.

In France, the Muslims must live their religion while at the same time respecting the laws of the French republic.

How?

Do you remember those Moroccan girls who came to school wearing scarves around their heads?

No, tell me about it.

Some teachers didn't want to admit them to classes, saying that, since France was a secular country, the pupils must not show their religious affiliation in school.

And so what happened?

There was a lot of discussion. Finally, some girls gave up wearing the scarf. Others were taken out of school by their parents. They were wrong to deprive their daughters of an education.

The other day on television I saw women covered from head to toe. They looked like ghosts.

What you saw were Afghan women whom men mistreat in the name of Islam.

Does Islam oblige a woman to cover herself entirely?

No. You're talking about a veil called a *hijah,* and a *chador* in Iran. What the Koran says is simple: a woman who is praying and thus speaking to God must cover her head and not wear garments that are close-fitting. We also find similar restrictions among the Christians and the Jews. If a woman is dressed provocatively, if she is wearing, for example, a miniskirt or a blouse that reveals her bosom, if her hair is undone, she is not admitted into a church or a synagogue. Muslim women have the right to enter a mosque, but they must not mingle with the men. This is to avoid disturbances and other objectionable behavior. A house of prayer is not a meeting place for the sexes.

So God speaks of the veil.

Yes. In Sura XXIV ("The Light"), verse 31, He recommends that women believers "lower their gaze" and "cover their breast with their veils." In Sura XXXIII, verse

59, He speaks to the Prophet as follows: "Say to your wives and your daughters, and to the wives of believers, let their outer garments fall low. Thus it will be easier for them not to be recognized, and they will not be insulted." This means that the wives of believers had to distinguish themselves from unvirtuous women.

Why does God speak of wives? Did the Prophet have several?

In Islam a man has the right to four wives. This is called polygamy.

I know. "Mono" means "one." "Poly" means "several." But that's not fair!

You're right, that's not fair. You know, if we read the Koran attentively, we realize it's impossible for a believing man and good Muslim to be polygamous, for it is said, "provided he loves them all equally," that is, being fair and equitable with each one. Which is impossible. You cannot be in love with four women at the same time. There will necessarily be some preference, and thus an injustice. Today, polygamy is on the way out, for women are gaining rights, not in all the Muslim countries, alas, but in certain ones, such as Tunisia, where polygamy is outlawed. Neither the veil, in that fashion of the Taliban, nor polygamy are now acceptable there.

The women rebelled, I hope!

Yes, but not all the time and not all of them at the same time. Fortunately, women's associations in the Muslim countries such as Egypt, Morocco, or Algeria are struggling for changes in family law and for women to have the same rights as men. It isn't easy, for even if the words of the law are changed, it would take time for ways of thinking to accept the upset in their habits. A good Muslim must be a just man, so he would have to accept women having the same rights as he does in everyday life. In Islam it is spelled out that no shame or modesty attaches to talk of sexuality. In Arabic we say, *"La haya'a fi dine."*

What does that mean?

It means Islam talks straightforwardly about the relations between men and women. When I was a teenager, I read a little book, *The Perfumed Garden.* It was written in the fifteenth century by a man of religion in Tunisia, Sheik Nafzawi. It's a sexual-education text for young Muslims.

Of course, it is written for both boys and girls. The sheik explains how to make love according to the recommendations of Islam.

Let's get back to history!

So, after the end of the Ottoman Empire, it was the turn of the Europeans to settle with their weapons in the countries where they had not been invited: the French landed in Algeria in 1830; the English in Egypt in 1882; after Tunisia, the French set up a protectorate in Morocco in 1912.

Why did they go into these countries?

It's what's called colonization. "Colonize" means "to set up colonies in foreign lands," that is, to occupy lands by force and to impose laws and rules on the population of these countries. It's domination.

It's unjust!

That's right, it's unjust. But what made the occupation of these Arab and Muslim countries possible was the decline they were going through. It's like a sick body that cannot defend itself and is invaded by other illnesses.

Did the people rebel?

Yes, after a few decades, they rebelled. The worst of these wars of independence was the one in Algeria between 1954 and 1962. There were hundreds of thousands of deaths on both sides, and then the French who had been born and lived in Algeria had to leave.

Did Islam play a part in these wars?

Yes. Islam as a religion and a culture brought unity to all the Arab fighters. It brought them solidarity. But the conflict was not changed into a war of religion. After the countries won their independence, they underwent political upheavals.

Day 9

Why are Muslims so violent?

Not all Muslims are violent. You must not generalize about these things. No religion is totally pacifist or totally bent on war. In the Koran you find many verses that extol love, justice, harmony, and peace among men, forgiveness and wisdom, and you also find verses that urge the Muslim to fight when circumstances demand it. There is violence everywhere. Furthermore, the Muslims no longer constitute an empire, as at the start of Islam. The Muslim community is scattered over all the continents. I do not think someone from China has the same idea of how to practice the Muslim religion as a Moroccan or an African or a convert from Europe. It is true that violence and wars took place after the Prophet's death. That happened because

Islam is not a religion cut off from everyday life. It is concerned with the behavior of men in cities, their morality, the organization and the leadership of their community. That is what is called politics. Thus, Imam Khomeini, the man who overturned the shah of Iran in 1978 and set up an Islamic republic, could say "Islam is politics or it is nothing." In this way Islam can control the life of the people more directly than does Christianity or Judaism. Starting from this, the door is open to struggle and violence. Politics is often a struggle for power. If the combat is done in the name of Islam, as was the case in Iran, the violence caused will necessarily be blamed on Islam.

Yes, I want to know and understand because people are now talking about Islam because of the attacks on September 11.

You're right. So be patient and go on listening to the history of Islam. Here I must tell you about a sect called the *hashashins*. (A sect is a group of people who blindly follow a leader called a "guru.") The Arabic word *hachiche* means "grass," and more generally "drug." The *hachachin* is a lover of drugs, someone who smokes hashish or marijuana. This sect lived in western Asia, that is in Syria and Persia in the eleventh and twelfth centuries. Its leader, Hassan al-Sabbah, a strict, harsh, and authoritarian Muslim, was nicknamed "the Old Man of the Mountain." (He died in 1166.) After he became a guru, he settled in the castle of Alamut, not far from the Caspian Sea, and there he sent off troops on punitive expeditions against the rulers. First, however, he drugged his followers with Indian hemp, or marijuana. He made kings and princes tremble with fear. His weapons were terror, hatred, and murders. The word *hashashins* has become the English word "assassins."

Was "the Old Man of the Mountain" also a bad Muslim?

He was a Shiite and wanted to remain a mystery. People who now commit terrorist suicide attacks have been compared to the disciples of the Old Man of the Mountain. But here again, this does not come from Islam.

I know. "Islam" means "submission to peace" and tells us not to commit crimes. But the people who've made these attacks are Muslims.

Yes, but not all Muslims are part of Islam.

What does that mean?

Not everyone who claims to belong to a religion belongs to it in the same way.

Okay. What happened next?

Islam spread a lot in Africa and Asia. (Did you know that the largest Muslim country is in Asia? It's Indonesia.) Can you imagine—there were a few hundred Muslims in the seventh century, and today there are more than a billion.

A billion Muslims in the world! Why have so many people become Muslims?

The Arabs are a minority compared to the Asians who are Muslims. And not all Arabs are Muslims. So you find Christian Arabs in Egypt—these are the Copts, who are about 15 percent of the population. And there in Lebanon, where they are Maronites. They say their mass in Arabic. It's very beautiful.

And in France?

Islam is the second largest religion in France. The number of Muslims is estimated to be four million; most of them are from North Africa, others are Turkish, black Africans, Pakistani, Egyptian, and so on. Because in Islam there is no clergy, there is no agreement on designating a representative of all the communities.

Do you think the Muslims and the Christians will agree to live in peace in France and elsewhere in Europe?

There is no war between the two religions. The Muslims in France are fortunate to live in a democratic country that guarantees them the right to practice their religion freely. But you must not forget that France is a secular country, meaning there is no state religion. All religions have the right to exist, but none may dominate the others. To sum up, I'll cite a verse of the Koran in praise of what is called intermarrying: "O you men in truth, We have created you out of a male and a female, and We have made you into peoples and tribes so that you may know one another" (Sura IL, verse 13).

I have heard certain words and would like to understand their meaning. Can you explain them?

Which words?

"Intégriste" [Fundamentalist].

According to the dictionary, this word is taken from the Spanish *integrista,* which means "member of a party wishing the state to be dependent on the church." However, in this idea there is the word *"intègre,"* which stands for something good. A person with integrity is loyal, faithful to his principles and values. The opposite of this is the word "corrupt." The corrupt person is someone who has sold himself, sacrificed his values and principles for money or some other self-interest.

But what does "integrist" have to do with Islam?

The Muslim extremists do not use this word to refer to their actions. On the other hand, this word has been used to refer to Catholics who want greater strictness in the practice of their religion. They want, for example, for the mass to be said in Latin and not in other languages. When some Muslims began demanding an Islam that was stricter, more faithful to the time when it was born, the press termed them *Intégriste* [Fundamentalist].

How do they define themselves?

They call themselves "Islamists." They call each other brothers. This comes from the first movement created in 1928 by an Egyptian schoolteacher, Hassan al-Banna, in a little Egyptian town, Ismailia, and the movement bore the name Muslim Brothers. Hassan al-Banna struggled against the decline of values and against the influence of the Europeans on the Muslims. He opposed the Egyptian nationalist party, the Wafd, which was working for a democratic and parliamentary political system. One of their leaders, Sayyid Qutb, was arrested and tortured for "plotting against Nasser," sentenced to death, and executed on August 29, 1966. It was his teacher, al-Banna, who said, "Every bit of land on which the flag of Islam has flown is for every Muslim a homeland that he must preserve, for which he must work and fight a holy war." The movement has made its way in Egypt and other Muslim countries. They are well organized, come to the aid of the poor and the ill, and guide themselves by the many books left by Sayyid Qutb, who was a well-educated man.

When we listen to the sermons of the Islamists, we understand that they are seeking to impose by force a way of life, of behavior, and of dress that rejects contemporary life. They have forgotten something simple: Islam came into being more than fourteen centuries ago. Its writings contain values that are valid for all time, eternally. But there are also things that were of concern at the time of its birth but that do not fit in with modern times. These people want to go back to the time of the Prophet and to take Muhammad's message in a very literal, schematic, and caricatural way.

For example?

The so-called Islamists do not want women to be the equals of men, nor for them to have rights, nor for them to decide their own fate. They are in favor of polygamy and repudiation.

What is "repudiation"?

The husband has the legal right to divorce his wife without asking her opinion and without consulting a judge or lawyer. He sees a public official for religious affairs and asks him to send a notice to the wife.

But that's unfair.

It's neither fair nor humane, but that's changing in some Muslim countries that want to be modern. Some people have the custom of saying to a woman: "You must obey your husband; if you don't have a husband, you must obey your father; if you don't have a father, obey your brother; and so forth." The women must not dress in certain ways. The men saying this refer to certain verses in the Koran that do not grant the same rights to women as to men, or to other verses that they interpret in a way that suits them. I hope that steps will be taken in the Muslim countries so that women will not be devalued and scorned in the name of Islam. A woman should be a man's equal. Those who maltreat women thus forget that God hates injustice and humiliation.

There are people who have certainly memorized the Koran, but remember only the verses whose literal sense suits them. Now, the Koran is open to many other interpretations. What is called fundamentalism does harm to Islam and to true Muslims.

Do they do this on purpose or are they not well educated?

The worst ones are "semi-educated."

What is "semi-educated"?

It refers to people who can read but do not understand what they are reading. They think they are learned although they are ignoramuses. Such people are dangerous.

The word "fundamentalist"?

It is like the word *"intégriste."* It means going back to the fundamental principles of Islam, as if the world had not undergone any change.

The word "jihad"?

It means "effort." The Muslims first understood it as "effort over oneself, resistance against temptation, against the attractions of evil." Later, it was used as an appeal to combat when the Prophet was threatened and persecuted by the people living in Mecca who did not believe in his message. After the Prophet's death, Islam's expansion was carried out by fighting. In the eleventh century, when the Christians decided to go off and make war against the Muslims, that is, to go on a "crusade," the

Muslims declared a *jihad,* a fight in self-defense against the aggressors. The word does not make good sense today, for Islam continues to spread peacefully and no one really threatens it. So the people who use the word today are guilty of a misrepresentation. They are trying to make other people afraid.

The word "fatwa"?

The word is derived from the word *fata,* which means "dictate." Here *"fatwa"* means "an opinion concerning religious matters," but it is not a law. It is expressed by someone who has a good knowledge of the Koran: a specialist, a teacher of religion. But when a *fatwa* is declared—for example, the order to go and kill a Muslim who has written or said things judged inadmissible—that is an abuse. Islam does not make a *fatwa* into a law or decree that must be carried out.

The word "shari' a"?

It's a line of conduct, a morality laid down by the ancients of the religion. It is based on the Koran and on the words of the Prophet. For some people, it's more than a morality, it's a juridical framework, that is, a set of laws that Muslims must apply in daily life. But the *shari'a* is not obligatory. Not all the Muslim countries apply it. For most of them it is a step backward that is incompatible with modern law and modern life.

The word "tolerance"?

The word "tolerate" means "to put up with, accept." In concrete terms, this means: "I am not like you, I am not of your religion, I am not of your country, I do not agree with your ideas, and still I accept you, that you practice your religion, speak your language, and think what you will. But in exchange you, too, must accept what I am." Tolerance has meaning only if it is mutual. Intolerance is not accepting and even rejecting those who are different from oneself. It fosters racism.

Must everything be tolerated?

No. We must not accept racism or humiliation.

What does "humiliation" mean?

Humiliating someone is making him feel ashamed, depriving him of his quality of being human, that is, his pride and dignity. It is to harm what he is, it is to do him evil and make him suffer injustices.

Is Islam a tolerant religion?

At the beginning, no religion is tolerant. Every religion seeks to convince people that it is unique and the only right one. But when we pay careful attention to sacred books like the Koran, we learn that Islam was not in favor of making war on the Jews and the Christians. So the Islam that recognizes the other religions and their prophets wishes to be tolerant. I'll quote three verses that prove that Islam is tolerant. Sura II, verse 256: "No constraint in religion," that is, people must not be compelled to convert to Islam. And people who are already Muslims must not be compelled to behave according to rules established by the force of a leader. Sura CIX, verse 6: "Your religion for you, my religion for me." It is clear: religious beliefs, like tastes and color preferences, are not to be the subject of dispute but of mutual respect. Sura XXVIII, verse 56: "It is not you who are to guide whom you will; it is God who guides whom he wills." The text is clear: Islam does not force anyone to believe in its message; everyone has the right to his own beliefs and to be respected, as he must respect the beliefs of others. Finally, no man has the right to take God's place and give the believers orders; in other words, those who proclaim themselves religious leaders of Islam are in error. There is no clergy in Islam, that is, intermediaries between God and man; there is no priest or rabbi as in other religions. There is no pope, that is, a supreme leader who would be God's representative on earth. There are imams, that is, qualified persons who preside at prayer and deliver sermons on Friday in the mosque. The imam has moral authority, but he does not play the same role as a priest or rabbi. But like other religions, Islam does have fanatics, people who do not tolerate those who do not think and believe the way they themselves do. They are a minority. Unfortunately, this minority is active and wicked. They do harm to Muslims and non-Muslims alike. The fanatics act in the name of Islam, but often they are people who are illiterate and have not studied the writings, or they are intelligent people who use Islam in order to spread political propaganda, that is, their own interests. These are the famous "semi-educated people." As one Tunisian poet put it, "Islam has its diseases." We are suffering from their effects. This takes us back to the start of this conversation: the attacks against Americans on September 11, 2001.

Why did they do that?

Because they think the Americans are responsible for the misery of certain Arab Muslim peoples. Because they have been led astray by leaders who think they are dispensing justice. Because they are mistaken and refuse to recognize it. Because they have been "worked over" by these same leaders, who have managed to stifle their thoughts and doubts. Because they were told that God loves martyrs and rewards them by sending them straight to heaven. Because they were not brought up to believe in tolerance and to respect the ideas and culture of others. Islam has never taught hatred, crime, or suicide; it punishes those errors very severely.

What is a "martyr"?

It is someone who dies "in the service of God." A martyr is a Muslim who dies in combat in the name of the faith to defend Islam when it is attacked, to defend himself if he is attacked as a Muslim, or to liberate his country from foreign occupation. There are two Arabic words for referring to a martyr: *fidâ î* ("he who offers his life") and *shahid* ("he who testifies"). God promises the martyr paradise.

What is the "Taliban"?

The Arabic word *talaba* means "to ask"; a *tâleb* is someone who claims knowledge, education. The word "Taliban" refers not to students but to a movement that claims to be religious. It first came from Afghanistan and is characterized by its hatred of women and art. The Taliban terrorize women, forbid them to go to school, to work in public administration, to engage in sports, to listen to music; when they fall ill, they are not cared for. The Taliban kill the women they judge "immoral," stoning them to death, and they bury alive couples judged guilty of adultery. These are the practices of another time: for example, cutting off the hand of thieves or executing in a stadium someone condemned to death who hasn't been tried in a court. They know a few verses of the Koran, but most of them can't read or write. And all this they do in the name of Islam!

They're crazy!

Yes, they are crazy and dangerous, ignorant and barbaric. They do not understand Islam or its civilization. If they were given complete freedom, they would permanently ruin the Islamic culture.

Is it true that painting is forbidden in Islam?

No, that's false. What is forbidden is representing God or the prophet Muhammad. We cannot draw their faces. God is a spirit. How could he be represented? As for Muhammad, it is his spirit that is essential. It can't be visualized. But we can draw anyone and anything else. In Persia, there is a very fine tradition of painting and drawing, some illuminations adorning the old manuscripts.

Now I understand! There is Islam and then there are Muslims. Some of them have understood the Prophet's message while others have misunderstood it or pretend to have understood it and want to go back in time. But tell me, can't we change things in Islam?

We are living in a modern era, so you want Islam to be adapted to this modern life. You're right. People who have tried to change things for the better—improving the conditions of women, for example—have met with a lot of difficulties. In Islam, as in other religions, there are things that are eternal and things that are temporary, that is, valid for one time period and not for all times. The problem is that some Muslims say that all of it is eternal and nothing must change; others say that this religion can be adapted to the time in which we are living. People have tried and failed to introduce freedom into certain Muslim countries, so how can you think of trying to change their religion? As I told you the other day, the most important, the most urgent thing is to make a clear separation between religion and politics. As long as the people who govern rely on religion, we will have problems and madnesses like fanaticism and what follows from it, that is, terrorism and ignorance.

For example?

Like other religions, Islam has not been much in favor of women being treated as the equal of men, even though it guarantees them certain rights. Today, Muslim societies feel the need to evolve. We tend to forget that Khadija, the Prophet's first wife, was a businesswoman, a tradeswoman doing a man's job. We can refer to her status, to her role, in order to reform the condition of women today. Islam does not prohibit laws giving women rights, but men have been afraid to establish equal rights between themselves and women. Only Tunisia has changed its laws for women so that they are better able to look out for themselves. In Saudi Arabia, women don't even have the right to drive an automobile. As for women in Afghanistan, they have had to suffer under the most barbaric laws, those of the Taliban. But the Taliban are men who have understood nothing of Islam and have distorted it, so much so that every Muslim community has suffered and goes on suffering from it. They have destroyed Buddhist statues several centuries old that were the legacy of all humankind.

What, then, should we do?

Struggle against ignorance. That is what makes people fanatical and intolerant. Nothing is more dangerous than someone who knows nothing and thinks he knows everything. Fortunately, Muslim women have set up associations to demand their rights. There's still a lot to do to achieve full justice.

How should we struggle?

We have to start with the schools. The girls should attend until they graduate, and refuse, for example, to be removed from school as soon as they are teenagers. In addition, Arab and Muslim countries should revise text-books in favor of greater tolerance and respect for human and women's rights, citing examples of great Muslim scholars who have promoted universal civilization. They should eliminate from these books examples favoring closed minds or suggesting to the child that it is normal for a man to hit his wife or that a woman should remain at home while the man works, and so forth.

Islam should be taught in the same way as other religions, and the truth should be told about its spread, which was not achieved without fighting wars. It should also be noted that times are changing and that it is not as if we were living in the time of the Prophet. In other words, while respecting the message of the Prophet and while believing in God, man has the right to change, that is, to adapt to modern times without giving up his beliefs and basic values. The child should be given every tool to help him make up his mind for himself. It is very important to give the child freedom so that he is not influenced by any particular religion. There is a huge amount of work to be done here, but we have to make a start. That is what we have just been doing.

Before bringing this conversation to a close, I will give you a list of words and you will tell me what they have in common:

admiral	chess	monsoon
alcohol	chive	mulatto
algebra	coffee	mummy
algorithm	crimson	muslin
almanac	cupola	orange
amalgam	divan	racket
amber	drug	rice
amulet	Eden	risk
apricot	emerald	saccharine
artichoke	fanfare	safari
azimuth	felucca	saffron
azure	gala	sandal
banana	gauze	sapphire
baroque	gazette	satin
benzine	giraffe	soda
benzoin	guitar	sofa
bergamot	hashish	sorbet
blouse	hazard	spinach
cable	jacket	sugar
caliber	jasmine	taffeta
camellia	lacquer	talc
camphor	lemonade	talisman
carafe	lilac	tariff
caravel	lute	tarragon
carousel	magazine	troubadour
check	mattress	x
chemistry	mohair	zenith

I don't know all these words, so I can't know what they have in common.

All these words and others I haven't mentioned originated in Arabic. Now they are used in the languages derived from Latin, and in other languages as well, and hardly anyone knows their origin.

Is the "x" also Arabic?

Curiously, that letter does not exist in the Arabic alphabet, but the Arab mathematicians called an unknown sum *chai* ("thing"), abbreviated to *ch*. Now, in old Spanish, the sign "x" corresponds to the sound "ch."

My, what a lot of things you know!

Not really, I found all these words in the dictionary. To conclude this discussion, I will give you two quotations from the prophet Muhammad (these words are called *hadits*):

"From cradle to grave, go in search of knowledge, for whoever longs for knowledge loves God."

"The study of science has the value of the fast, the teaching of science has the value of a prayer." The Prophet considered the acquisition of knowledge as important as the two pillars of Islam: the fasting during Ramadan and the daily prayers.

Index